And so it begins…

I've done the deed. After 24 years at the chalk face, I have decided to leave teaching and set up my own business in glamping - well, Shepherds' huts glamping to be precise. Actually glamping is the understatement. Pure unadulterated luxury I'd say. It's going to be quite a journey.

1

This epiphany of an idea came about due to a number of circumstances. Firstly, I had to escape. I'm the last member of the 'old dinosaur' club. 7 ladies, all teachers - all but me had escaped. I was the eternal sparrow at the window. At 46 years of age I felt almost tangible fear of another 21 years of paper work, assessments, meetings, observations, feedback, marking, the long walk to the head teacher's office … (the teaching part is the smallest of fragments of the job and the bit I enjoy) before my pension kicked in. I felt sure that death would catch me first. It was time to go.

Secondly, I live in heaven. Morndyke is our family farm- small: 65 acres on site, 2 of which are an established course fishing lake - but truly beautiful. We are in the heart of North Yorkshire - pure 'White Rose' country. James Herriot is our God and master (well, according to my mother anyway...). Thirsk is 3 miles away. We are not in the dales, nor the moors, but within spitting distance of both. I wake each morning and rest my eyes on the Hambleton Hills in the distance, Sutton Bank scored on the horizon, unbroken views an arm's stretch away. At the moment, the cooler mornings are still, with the dew touching the growing hay and the sun, in all its glory, rising like a God over the hills. The oystercatchers are back, with their shrill cries, circling the fields. The sound carries me back to halcyon days. Our farm is my little piece of heaven.

Thirdly, I've never been considered 'normal'. I wouldn't know normal if I fell over it. 'Normal' would be living and working and socialising and make up and gym membership and handbags. My world is a little different. Whilst typing this, my two turkey poults: Mary and Gabrielle (5 weeks old), are making themselves busy cleaning up the floor with their beaks on the one hand, and decorating it from their other end on the other hand. The cat, Kiki is sat in the laundry basket, kneading the clean, freshly washed and dried dressing gown of my daughter, and has just been joined by Khufu, the other cat. They presumably have taken refuge from the sharp little beaks of the poults. There were three. Elizabeth passed away three days ago. I miss her. Turkeys share their love of dying with sheep. Hobbies include shitting, sleeping in my hair and dying – well making every effort to do so. Apparently everything is food. I extracted something unmentionable out of Mary's posterior the other day - part of my rug. The vet has already been called out, the turkeys have been injected every day this week after their chest infections and gastrointestinal infections took hold. However I adore them. Alan tolerates them. Alan is long suffering and reasonably patient. There is a definite pecking order here. I do wonder sometimes, why he married me. In his previous life, no animals entered the house. Now he has had to put up with cats, turkeys and sheep all sharing from time to time. He drew the line (strangely) at hens. Something passed his lips about 'wringing their bloody necks if another hen comes through that door.' Thankfully it was hens and not poultry he mentioned...

Snowberry, Willow and Buckthorn

I have three cows, namely Snowberry, Willow and Buckthorn. Alan would contest the ownership status. However, he was foolish enough to 'lend' me these three bovines quite a number of years ago when they were each a mere 6 months old. At the time I needed serious lawnmower power to graze the land my horses were on - what better munching machines than three growing 'fatteners' (the colloquial and rather grim term used to describe cows that are eventually destined for the nation's dinner plate) to eat down the emerald green, lush Spring grass? Alan assumed, quite wrongly, that he would be receiving three fat 'oven ready' cows back, but by that time I had named them. The power of a name - my theory is once it is named, it is safe. I am a hardened vegetarian and spend my life rescuing life's desperate cases. Alan didn't know this at the time. He does now. Most of his 'Suckler' cows (our breeding stock) now have names. Snowberry, Willow and Buckthorn, with a bit of gentle persuasion, were promoted into the Suckler herd. Result.

My three bovine babies are full of character, and have three very different personalities. Snowberry is the eternal mother, gentle, sweet-natured and friendly; Buckthorn has a kind eye and is friends with those that spend time with her. She knows what she likes and likes what she knows. Willow is more aloof and will honour me with her presence if there is something in it for her, but she is happy and accepts me as part of the herd. All three come when they are called by name and have a ponchance for bread, barley, grass - in fact any food that is considered a sweetie in cow terms. They have grown, matured, had babies and are part of our 32 strong breeding cows that run with our pedigree

Limousine bull (Hercules). The herd's offspring make up about another 70 'beasts' - as they are affectionately named.

To maintain a healthy herd, there are certain things that need to happen - daily, monthly or yearly. One of these yearly events is a 'big un' - the visit of 'Dan-the-foot-trimming-man'. Dan Kitching is a legend of a fellow. He appears around Easter every  year with his space age equipment and calmly, sensitively and professionally coerces the cattle down the race into a crush. With the press of a few buttons and levers, the cows are clamped, lifted and rolled onto their sides whilst he works his magic on their feet.

As you can imagine, it is not the favourite pastime of a cow to be so treated. The wily old girls hang back, plant their feet and refuse to budge. None more so than 'T'oad Gran' - our oldest girl and possibly the oldest cow in England. At a grand old age of 23, she has been there, done that many times. She lives out her days as the matriarch and shows the young cows how to avoid the crush. She has done her job well. This year, we had the bright idea of segregating a section of the herd into a temporary pen to free up a bit of space in the waiting area. Alan happened to be really quite poorly so wasn't on top form. He persuaded a section of the herd into the pen, and then got about the task of shifting cows towards 'Dan-the-foot-trimming-man' and his crush. All was going well with not too much blue language occurring, when an almighty crash resounded around the fold yard. 'What the...?' Before the sentence could be completed, a vision appeared of about 10 cattle stampeding with gates flying, hooves in the air, bellowing, 10 tonnes of moving beef careered in all directions. SHIT! The temporary pen was no more. The red and white cow had happened to be in the temporary pen. The same cow that is claustrophobic, the same cow that is never penned for any reason, the same cow that had a 5 bar gate now wrapped round her neck. The fold yard, incidentally, is next to the fishing lake, where it happened to be a perfect fishing day, and a number of older gentlemen had decided to quietly pass the time away. All came to investigate but were met with a wall of rampaging cows. Insurance claims, air ambulances, fire-brigades all flashed in front of my eyes. I ran. God, how I ran. I didn't know I still could. I appeared to be fleeing the scene. This is slander and in fact I was heading for the gate to close off the yard. I made it in time for the moving wall to screech to a stop in front of me. Hercules, blowing like a demon, was heading the charge. Flanking him, the 'cow with no name that can't be penned' - however her future is now secured: 'That red and white bastard' is the name that Alan has chosen for her.

Two bulls together- Alan and Hercules

After the cattle were returned, peace was restored, and 'Dan-the-foot-trimming-man' continued. All went well for the rest of the day, and all the cattle had their pedicures.

Snowberry was due to calve imminently. 'Dan-the-foot-trimming-man' took this into account and was even more careful and gentle. For the rest of the week, I kept a close eye on her, and then three days later this happened:

God bless you Snowberry.

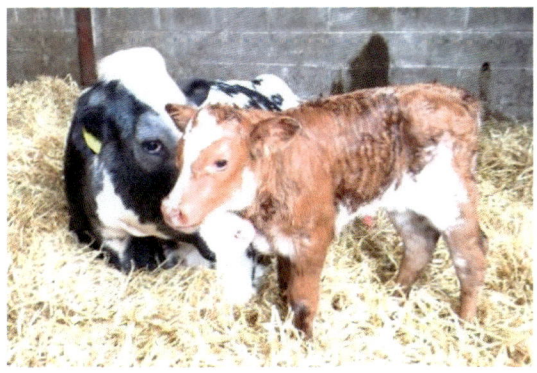

Farriers, Physios, Fangs and Fame

I have a weakness. Horses. Since I took my first breathe, these became my nemesis. The amount of money spent, hardship felt, and both physical and mental pain fashioned by these creatures is insurmountable. I think I could have paid off the national debt if I had ploughed the same amount of cash into it as I have on my horses. I suspect there is many a vet whose children have had the privilege of a private education on the back of my equine bills. But it's in the blood. Simple. No amount of therapy or broken bones will cure that one, we are inescapably entwined.

My horse, Capote (Ca- poe –tay) is a stunning Spanish PRE – a pure blooded, hot headed, fire storm of a horse; deeply sensitive,

spiritual, charismatic, with a plethora of emotions and expressions. Routines need to be firmly established, behaviour patterns negotiated, and as all Yorkshire men acknowledge: he 'likes what he knows and knows what (or whom) he likes - and is not backward in coming forward in telling me. One might even stretch to a diagnosis of autism - he is that 'Yorkshire'- a true Yorkshire Spaniard. He was brought over from Spain as a 'backed' but unbroken four year old. He still bears the scar on his nose that Spanish pure-breds carry - from the serrated blade used to 'encourage' a perfect head carriage. Fashion is a cruel friend for horse and human alike.

Capote is my soul mate, my best friend and he will stay by my side for the remainder of our days – until whichever of us will meet our maker first. There is a very real likelihood that it will be me, as riding him is like mounting a nuclear warhead. As one highly skilled 4* eventer commented, approaching a fence on him was like flooring a Ferrari. I know the feeling well. He is

Bishop Burton BE 90 2015

everything I dreamed of, from the days of childhood to the creeping oppression of middle age. Quite simply, he is perfect.

My dream from the earliest of my memories, in the days of 'Sundancer and Anna', was to follow the footsteps of the famous: Lucinda Green, Ginny Elliot, Princess Anne and become an eventer. Nothing beats, or even comes close to the thrill of flying a horse over fences cross country. The feeling of two hearts, one body, wind-whipped tears and thundering hooves, then no  but suspension of flight and pure energy as the ground fast approaches before the thunder returns. In my dreams I fly the 4*s of Badminton and Burghley, but in my waking life I struggle, with my heart in my mouth, over the BE90s. I will never be more than the sum of my total, but that is far better than being the sum of missed opportunities. I have my horse. He flies with me. He breaks my bones, he empties my purse. He sees me and calls to me. There is nothing that comes close.

Capote lives in our little herd consisting of Casey Jones — a neurotic, effeminate, Welshman (Section B for those in the know) and Tara, my mother's Welsh Section D-cross matriach. I swear the cross is guinea pig. They have their place and hierarchy, and Tara keeps the boys in check. They love her really. Maintaining the herd is a life's work. Farriers call every 6 weeks, an equine physiotherapist every 3 months, and dentist every 9 months. Not to mention the vet. Or the instructors, who stand hand on hips, pained expressions and feighned tolerance as we negotiate the complexities of dressage or leap like kangeroos over showjumps. I *will* make it to Badminton, I will. The mantra resounds round the fog of my brain. Left rein, right leg, shoulder in, don't fall out, talk through the bit, look to the bend, more impulsion,

forward the trot. The instructions rattle like machine gun bullets. I *will* make Badminton, I will. Even if I *am* just a spectator…

Horses are high maintainance – in every sense. I am blessed with

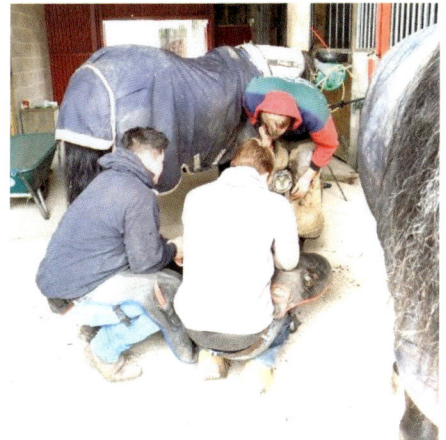 a team of highly skilled professionals that keep me sane. Huw Dyer and his lads are the farriers of choice that any horse would dream of. They are kind, incredibly

talented perfectionists, where nothing is too much trouble. I would be lost without them , as would my horses hooves. They appear like Mr Ben, every 6 weeks with smiles and banter and work their magic. The saying is so true – no foot, no 'oss. These boys know their onions. The young lads learn their trade from the boss, who guides and steers them under watchful eyes.

Then there is Tim Jarman. I envy my horse. Tim has magic hands. Once every three months Capote has the luxury of Tim's hands. He irons out knots and loosens tightness, strokes and pummels and pulls and twists. I stand, holding the end of a lead rope, feeling more tight and twisted and knotted and sore as he works. Capote breaths and sinks and smiles and sleeps. I'm not surprised. In my next life, I'm coming back as my horse.

I perhaps don't envy the visit from the dentist. Dan Astle-Carter is a gentle, sensitive and intuitive professional that wheels a

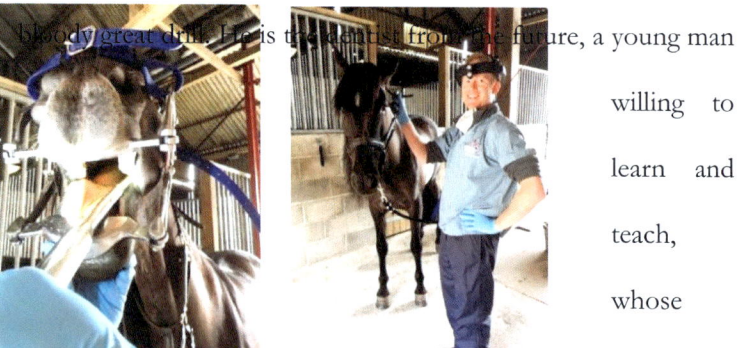

bloody great drill. He is the dentist from the future, a young man willing to learn and teach, whose holistic belief has changed the future for my horses. Before the days of Dan, Casey Jones was in trouble. His mouth was buggered. Years of dentistry from charletons had taken their toll. Case was doomed. Dan and his drill then performed their miracle, now Case, Capote and Tara have filmstar smiles. Dan is another of my equine heros.

The vets that keep the horses fine-tuned are the famous crew from Skeldale: Peter Wright, Julian Norton, Helen, Tim and Sarah all have casted their experienced gaze upon my four-legged friends. I love them and trust them. They are simply the best. The Yorkshire Vets are aptly named. Genuine and gorgeous just as the programme portrays, these highly skilled professionals poke orifices, stick in needles, cogitate and collaborate. Their touch is gentle and their knowledge is strong. My horses are safe in their hands.

It has long been said that Capote has film star looks. I think so. No rose-coloured glasses can deceive the eye. He is utterly lovely. The team from the Yorkshire Vet television series thought so too and he appears in his cameo role in series one, but then took centre stage in series four (episode four) when my poor baby developed a rash. Only Capote could do this in such style. Not one or too concealable blobs, but a monumental array of lumps. Small pox would have looked better. We evented at Bishop Burton Horse Trials amongst quizzical gazes, as onlookers stared at this spotty oik. No tossing mane and snorting fire dragon, just spots. Lots of spots. As we jogged around and stormed the fences, gasps of awe and wonder filled my mind. Indeed there were gasps - of shock and horror. Capote had acne. Months ensued of vets and examinations, prodding and poking, allergy responses and money. The film crew pricked up their ears. My chance of fame – of Badminton and Burghley and 4* and … spots. The episode is aired next week. I await with bated breathe. I love my horse, spots and all. After all the money and tests and stress, a simple packed of anti-histamines did the trick. Good old eBay.

Talking Turkey.

As I sit writing this blog, with Gabrielle on my knee, slowly being lulled to sleep by the repetitive sounds of the keyboard, it occurs to me that perhaps I live a life less ordinary. I'm not too  sure where I fit into the grand scheme of things. To me, working on a computer with one of my turkeys 'helping' is all part and parcel of life.

I do however, smile to myself when I'm tutoring maths to a group of children, and Mary decides to have a wander over the table, usually defecating at the most inopportune moment on some hard fought reasoning problem - as if to pass judgement. Gabrielle will then make a monumental effort to fly onto the table to join her sister, sending papers and children scattering to the four winds. 'Oh nooooo,' they admonish as I extract turkey, poo and papers from the far reaches of the kitchen. 'Not to worry...' I smile and continue – the kitchen towel slowly diminishing as each poo is negotiated and niftily swept into the bin. Maths at Morndyke is never boring. The cats don't help. Khufu stares and sits on papers, refusing to budge an inch. Kiki, on the other hand, has developed a rather naughty habit of sniffing said turkeys rather too closely. I have then witnessed the sniff turn into subtly opened jaws that close around their scrawny necks, only to be accompanied with an alarm call of a rather surprised chick. Usually a swipe with the back of my hand is enough to displace the cat. It leaves me with an uneasy feeling that perhaps I should change the turkey flavoured cat food to a different brand.

The same thing happened when we had the lambs in the house. Juno and Jupiter joined us at a couple of days old. I zipped them in my coat, brought them home, and then lo and behold, they had moved in. The kitchen transforms into a sanctuary with every new arrival. The lambs wore nappies through the duration of their stay. I have never known an animal make so much mess. Who would have thought that two little pet lambs, no bigger than the cats could wee so much? However, they soon outgrew

the kitchen as they stretched their legs. They rapidly realised that

the world spread beyond the confinement of the room. It soon

became a race once that kitchen door was opened. Slippy tiled

floors gave no grip to cloven hooves. The lambs would wheel

spin out of the door into the study, displacing flying cats. All

four were quicker than me. All four claimed ownership of the

sofa. I was relegated to the rug. I knew things weren't quite

right, but I couldn't quite put my finger on it…

The lambs nearly finished Alan off. 'Those bloody sheep should

be outside,' he would cry,' there is shit all over the place.' – A despairing wail would crack his tone. It was lucky he was out at work every day. We all soon learnt to scarper pretty damn quick when the familiar rumble of his Toyota and trailer cruised into the yard. It's amazing how quick one can sweep up poo and place distractions over wet carpets...

I had to give Alan time. He was emotionally scarred.

However time is a great healer and the stress of sharing his house with two renegade sheep paled into the background. The dust settled, the cats took therapy and the carpets slowly recovered. And then Christmas happened.

Behind the farm is a disused air base - a relic from the Second World War. It is peppered with derelict old buildings that were once occupied by the Canadian air force. The land is vast and open – perfect for landing bombers and spitfires, perfect for turkey farms. I struggle with the concept of factory farming, all our stock are farmed with love and are free range. I spend my time rescuing misshapen and unloved creatures. However, on the air base there happens to be a number of turkey factory farms dotted around the 3.5 mile track. I ride Capote regularly around the base, negotiating startled partridge and indignant skylarks, with the odd feed lorry thrown in for good measure. I remember it was cold two weeks before Christmas – as one would expect. Capote and I trotted merrily along, putting the world to rights – he's a great listener, when I happened upon a turkey hut. Now Christmas was a mere snip away, and there, in front of me was an open door. From behind the screens, babbles of tiny voices filtered through. As did a turkey. An oven ready, white, fat and heavy bird with the innocence of a baby – indeed they are butchered at 16 weeks old. I froze. So did Capote. A thousand thoughts flooded my brain as time stood still. A baby. A Christmas dinner gazed up with child-like eyes. What could I do? What could anyone do? The only choice was to kidnap said turkey. I jumped off Capote, who snorted and backed off at high speed. I knew that turkey napping was not strictly legal, so having a horse turn into a boggle-eyed, fire-breathing, snorting dragon right next to where I was about to commit a heinous crime was not ideal. Turkey or horse, turkey or horse? Turkey won. Capote snapped his bridle and buggered off. Shit. Quick as a flash, I grabbed the turkey who was rather alarmed at the prospect of being free one minute, then encased in my arms the next. She did what any self-respecting turkey would do and shouted loudly, which clearly was terrifying for the boggle-eyed, fire-breathing dragon of a horse. I held her beak closed between finger and thumb, tucked her under my arm and caught Capote. Thankfully he followed like a lamb, the turkey realised actually it was quite a warm, snug place to be and fell asleep. However, I now had quite a trek home – 1.5 miles with an enormously heavy sleeping turkey and a meek and gentle horse in tow. I called her Mary.

 As we walked, I noticed in the distance a lorry, slowly growing larger. I recognised it - a turkey collection lorry heading straight for Mary's hut. Oh shit. 1 loose horse, 1 rider on foot and 1 large turkey fast asleep. As it approached, I smiled and waved and walked on. I was thrown a quizzical glance and

then the lorry stopped and pulled up, 50 yards behind me at the turkey hut. I felt sick at the thought of the 'what ifs?' At least Mary was safe. I owe someone for a turkey.

Mary was hilarious, clearly Rod Hull had had a turkey when he created 'Emu', she entertained me for hours with her antics. I loved her, but something was missing from her life. She had spent all her short days being intensively farmed with a thousand other turkeys. She was now on her own and had no one to talk turkey to. I needed another turkey. The hunt was on.

Bird flu had struck. All sales and movement of poultry were banned. You try finding a live turkey over the Christmas period  too. Plenty offered me them, but sadly none were breathing. Many phone calls ensued and reconnaissance missions were undertaken but to no avail. Time was ticking. Eventually, after endless hours of enquiries, I found a man with a bird. At last, Mary was to have a friend. I had found Josephine. She was a very different bird to Mary – slightly coy but rather maternal. On her first night in the hen house, I found 3 old hens poised precariously on top of each other, under her wing. She looked slightly bemused, but accepted her new role as surrogate mother to a bunch of ageing ladies. Mary and Josephine clicked, and chortled merrily to each other whilst going about their daily business. They lived happily together for a couple of months, then Mary became ill. She sadly passed away in my mother's arms one winter's day. She left a huge hole in my life. Who would haver thought a scraggy, Christmas dinner would have so much heart and life? I missed her terribly, as did Josephine.

Again, I was left with one lonely turkey. This time it was  Josephine's turn. The loneliness of being the last turkey became a real problem for her and she pined. She became quiet, depressed and sedentary. As soon as she saw me, she would crouch down and gape her beak. Nothing could persuade her to come round. I took her to the vets on several occasions, who prodded, poked, injected etc, but to no avail. They came out on site – as did the film crew for 'The Yorkshire Vet'. I think a depressed turkey was a novelty for them. Her condition didn't alter. I even looked into the possibility of turkey anti-depressants, but funnily enough, there are no such things... I was at a loss as to what to do. The only option was more turkeys. The hunt was on (again).

Bird flu was still in full swing, so no turkeys could be traded. My previous lead had run dry. Then someone advised me to contact the turkey hatchery who produce thirty thousand chicks a week. Surely they could spare one? After a few false starts and some skulduggery, I managed to  'acquire' three newly hatched babies. My heart melted and I was in love. Mary (2), Gabrielle and Elizabeth were born. My babies imprinted on me and I on them. They are my shadows, but by God, they can shit. Poor Alan. Once again our house smells like a muck heap, chicks fly everywhere, cats scatter, poo is flung – chaos is resumed.

The three little bundles of fluff grew. They spend their evenings buried under my hair, or sleeping, or dust bathing on my chest. I am the archetypal mother hen and I love it. The cats sort of do. Alan doesn't.

My heart was broken again one morning when Elizabeth grew ill. She was quiet and subdued. I called out the vets, who injected, poked and prodded. But she was so young and so little. She had waited for me and died in my arms. Again, a gaping hole was left in my heart. I think of Mary (1) and Elizabeth and hope they are together now.

The two chicks (poults) grew and grew, and were still shitting, eating, dust bathing, chortling, chasing cats and scavenging. That's when Gabrielle had her accident. It happened so quickly and it was so horrific. She happened to have discovered the dish washer. Inside was a vast array of potential food. Bits of left overs adorned the base, and she was quick. As was the sprung loaded door. Life turned into slow motion as events unfolded themselves infront of my eyes – closing door, turkey head, gap closing, turkey not moving, door closing, door closing, door closing. BANG. Shit. Shit. Shit. I grabbed the door, yanked it open and pulled out a rather stunned turkey. She

was alive. How, I don't know. She should have been decapitated. The force of that door is huge and her head was near the hinge. I held her tight into my chest and didn't look or let go for an hour. I couldn't. I felt sick to my core. She felt rather dazed. I called the vets (again) and discussed turkey brain surgery, haemorrhaging, head aches.They said time would tell. She

moved rather slowly that evening – as if her world had slowed to half speed. I watched and waited and cuddled and paced. Time.That was the only answer. In time she recovered. She is slightly wary of dishwashers, but not of peas – her and Mary's favourite food. They still spend the evening flat out on my shoulders, but I've started to introduce them to the great outdoors. They are finding it great fun. I am trying to. Fledging turkeys and children is not an easy task.

Alan's Big Hole

There are certain things every boy loves, not least, holes. They love digging and moving shed loads of soil – but not by hand, I hasten to add. Give a boy a digger and he is happy. One of the curious aspects of life is that boys never change. Their needs and desires stay straight and steady from cradle to grave. Alan is no exception. He had been looking for an excuse to spend a handsome amount of money on a new digger for a significant amount of time. I gave him the perfect excuse. Glamping. To me, glamping meant romantic little shepherds' huts, nestled as if from a scene from 'The Fairy Caravan', with high spec interiors and furnishings to die for. To Alan it meant holes. No wonder he  was so keen on the idea. Before I had barely finished uttering the 'G' word, he was on the phone and it was ordered. A brand new red and black one. Don't ask me the spec; it had a couple of shiny buckets, lots of knobbly levers and a cab. What more could a man want? All his birthdays had come at once. I didn't see Alan after that. In the distance I heard the faint drone of an engine, and above the hedges I could just make out a metal boom. And boy, what a hole he dug. It could have swallowed the Eiffel Tower. Admittedly, thoughts did cross my mind that were rather naughty. It involved the hole, a trap and a belligerent old man – but that is another story. Alan kept digging. At one point, I did wonder if he had plans to drill for oil, but at last his hole was dug – 9 foot deep and wide – perfect to fit in the water treatment plant for the shepherds' huts. I praised his digging skills, and looking rather pleased, he commenced the concreting and back filling. Great. Job done. Or so I thought. What followed was a week of trench warfare. Across the growing haylage field appeared a torrent of moles. Big, athletic, tunnel-digging brutes, that left a trail of destruction. Upon closer

 inspection, these moles were very clever and accurate – their tunnel was straight and true and headed straight for the

ditch that drained the field ultimately into the Swale. On closer inspection, out of the tunnel came a black pipe – 5 feet deep and straight as a die from the tank. I wondered where Alan had been

So at last, the project was underway, the drains were in, and the grumbling about cost had commenced. But the digger stood idle. However, I had a plan. It involved horses.

For many a year I have pestered, nagged and moaned at poor Alan for an arena. My eventing dreams were always a finger-tip away when I was competing against the pros. The big names in the business start their youngsters in the same classes I fumble my way through. They have the advantage of not only years of experience; personal skill and high class horses; teams of professionals at their beck and call; bottomless pits for pockets - they also have arenas. Many hours are spent on artificial surfaces coercing horses to do their bidding. Whereas I fly with eyes closed and teeth clenched on muddy wintered grass and sun baked concrete clay trying to convince Capote that we are in the same league as the Olympic riders. He doesn't believe me. My dressage is not my best phase. A basic 40m x 20m arena costs somewhere between 30 and 50 thousand pounds for a contracted company to install– a laughable amount for any man, but hilarious to a Yorkshire farmer, hence the years of fruitless pestering. Alan had pacified me by getting planning permission, fencing the arena (no issue for a fencing contractor - which is his main job) and had prepared the base. This alone was a massive and expensive job – I knew this, as I had been told many a time. But now we stood still. The arena was worse than useless – covered in washed quarry stone 6 inches deep that no horse could work on. I knew I was asking for the moon. Each birthday and Christmas, my list was drawn – arena as number one, professional show jumps at number two. My list never went further – I thought it would be prudent to leave the 7.5 tonne lorry for another time…

Now Alan had a new digger, everything had changed. For the first time, the prospect of spending 2 days laying sand and the specially recycled shredded carpet known as 'clopf fibre' seemed attractive to him. I took advantage of the situation and struck like a cobra. The timing couldn't have been better. The lorries that were to deliver the loads had to have the ground as dry as snuff in order to avoid getting stuck, the cattle had to be out, the harvest not yet ready, even the money had been saved; Alan was fast running out of excuses. So reluctantly, with the enticement of two whole days playing diggers, Alan agreed. I wasted no time; urgent phone calls were made to Martin Collins Arenas. The sand and fibre were ordered. I watched the heavens with bated breath – if it rained it was game over. The Gods smiled down on me and the weather held. 9 eight-wheeler lorries rumbled into the yard, turned in the very dry field, and off loaded their cargo in the arena. It took two days for the men to dig and level and spread and harrow

and roll. At last it was done. I had an arena. My life was complete. Capote was very impressed and took full advantage of his new playground – as did I.

To Mull and Back

Once in a while, or so they tell me, it's good for the soul to take a holiday. This year, our annual pilgrimage took us up to the beautiful Scottish island of Mull. When I say us, I had better

clarify. 'Us' is the generic term for myself, the two kids and my father. Alan decided a year ago that holidays weren't really his thing. We all tended to agree after witnessing him morosely staring at fence posts and lovingly describing their intricate details on our last jaunt up to Scotland a year ago. He also disappeared for a day on the same said holiday to mournfully watch the local farmers bring in their harvest. Little comments, touched with sadness, escaped his lips about how the barley should be ready to combine at home. His eyes took on that faraway look as he lost himself in balers, combines and corn trailers. We all ardently agreed that this year, he would be far better off staying at home and taking care of the menagerie. He didn't argue. So, with (fleetingly) heavy hearts, we packed up the car, kissed all the animals, said our goodbyes and set off.

Now, to paint a picture of the situation, my father is a stickler for an itinerary. Having been a teacher all his life, the all-important detailed plan including minute by minute schedules needed adhering to - to the letter. Set off time was scheduled for 8am. However, my father had been a primary school teacher. He had not taught teenagers. Anna, my 11 year old-going-on-17-year-old had not been listed in the risk assessments. Thomas, my 10 year old, was not the issue. It was a Goliath of a task, and one that I had been bracing myself for - to ensure my daughter was ready on time. Up, breakfasted, and dressed on a non-school day was no mean feat for a nocturnal teenager. I had paled slightly and made a huge effort to hide the crack in my voice when Dad had gone through the itinerary. I mentally reorganised my morning and rescheduled my alarm for an hour earlier. I had to get up, muck out, feed up, sort out livestock, finish packing, and ensure the kids were ready. Sweat beaded on my forehead as the clock slowly and relentless ticked. I worked like a machine and made it.

My father had quite sensibly arranged for me to go on his car insurance so we could share the arduous journey. I decided, due to past history of having a tendency to fall asleep at the wheel on long journeys, to drive first. Fine - should be easy enough - except Dad's car is an automatic. And he is rather car proud. And I had filled it with 'essentials' – mucky wellies, blankets that had previously been play mats for the turkeys (I had shaken off the poo), and kids. And there was no clutch or proper gear stick. I think a woman's brain never shuts off, especially a mother's. My brain turned somersaults as I negotiated a new driving style, ticked off all the jobs that had needed doing, mentally counted in wellies, children, and other essentials and set off - on time too. I prided myself on my organisational skills. 10 minutes down the road, I was still head counting and assessing. Shit. Anna's bag. I had left it on my bed for her to add in her sponge bag. School boy error. There was no chance that bag was in the car. I pulled over. Dad looked horrified and checked the time. 'Anna's bag is on my bed' I gravely announced. Strange undistinguishable noises emitted from the back of the car that sounded something like 'it's not-my-fault-and-how-was-I-supposed-to-know-I-was-to-bring   my-bag-with-everything-I could possibly-need-in-it'. I turned round and headed back. 10 minutes back, then another 10 minutes to reach the same point again. 10 minutes into a 10 hour journey, the schedule was ruined. It didn't bode well. Dad, to give him credit was remarkably calm. I think there comes a time when you know you have lost. However, I wasn't going to let him down. I prayed the traffic police were still in bed and put my foot down. Dad's car cruises and we purred along like a pro. Somehow I made up the time before sleep took over and we swapped drivers. I'm still nervously watching for the post every morning though…

10 hours later we arrived, like refugees, at the cottage we were to

stay in, in Tobermory. It was quite lovely and the holiday was a great break. Dad had organised the days like a military operation, and, in true old boy style, had

written important information on the backs of endless envelopes. I photographed them just to make sure they were immortalised before inevitably getting lost... Day 1 – arrive; Day 2 – trip to

Fionnphort in order to island hop to Iona, then further hop to Staffa to see Fingal's Cave with its basalt columns, minke whale on the way and the puffins popping up like 'splat – a – rat' upon the hill side cliff face. Sounds straightforward? It certainly would be in under normal circumstances, if a little ambitious. Mull is a stunning island 50-60 miles long with approximately 2.5 thousand natives. This number swells exponentially during peak season. The roads on Mull are a throw-back to a bygone era. There is one stretch of 'normal' 2-way traffic; the rest is single track with numerous passing places. As one can imagine, a 60 mile trip from the north to the south of the island takes a bit of negotiation with oncoming tourists and disgruntled locals. 2 hours later we arrived. I was green. I'm not a great traveller, and my dad is not the most patient driver on the road; 0 -60mph, then 60-0mph every few hundred yards accompanied with 'sorry' or 'oh shit'. Staffa was incredible, but I declined the offer to return later in the week.

The journey back from Fionnphort to Tobermory was interesting. It was late and thankfully most tourists had found the local drinking houses. It was Sunday followed by Bank Holiday Monday. At 4pm Mull closed down. We had just nicely set off when Dad noticed the petrol gauge. Well, it was hard to miss. A large sign flashed 'low fuel'. No problem. My cars can do at least 50 miles at this point, and there were two petrol stations enroute. The first was where we were – Fionnphort, but the time was 5pm. Closed. Dad did a dad-type reconnaissance to plead with a local, but no joy. We set off. The journey back was far more sedentary, we travelled at a pleasant speed, which I thought was very thoughtful of Dad. He had fallen silent. The roads were empty. Perfect. The scenery was spectacular. Bleak mountains soared like Gods flanking the road. Golden eagles, white tailed eagles and buzzards cried above us. Ravens hugged the mountain tops and red deer looked upon us with questioning eyes. Dad slowed down. I appreciated the opportunity to drink in the vista. Dad checked the fuel: empty in 19 miles. We had 45 miles to go. No problem, I smiled, I am in the RAC, and there were worse things that could happen. I checked my phone. No service. Oh. I thought once we'd passed the mountains, service would resume. The mountains go on a long way. More than 19 miles. Silence fell like the clouds around us. Not one other human anywhere. No houses, no cars, no mad mountain running men. Nothing apart from the haunting cries of the raptors gathering. Dad slowed down. The midges sped up as if sensing the imminent stranding of their dinner. We slowly crawled our way for miles. It's amazing how far a car will run on fumes. At last we trailed limply into Craignure, the town central on the island. One petrol station - Closed. There was no chance of reaching Tobermory. We were stranded. We fought the midges and made our way to the pub. It seemed like a good idea. Matt and Amy were the two landlords and what angels they were. They took us under their wing, syphoned fuel from their own vehicles, called upon their mates to do the same and sent us merrily on our way. We are forever in your debt Matt.

The holiday continued without too many more mishaps; sunshine and showers, boat trips and wildlife tours ensued. It was a truly lovely holiday. Thanks Dad.

On arriving home, I had kissed the animals hello, started unpacking, and organising the kids to do the same, and then I met Alan. He seemed none the worse for wear. The animals were still alive - I call that a success. However, the bedroom smelt a little odd. I mused upon the cause and wondered upon its whereabouts, when Alan confessed to a terrible thing. Time stood still again. I stared at him. At least I knew he hadn't missed me. The tell-tale stain of debauchery, brown upon my bed. I thought the least he could have done was change the sheets, but no.

At least it was only the beer he had spilt whilst watching TV in bed. I'll buy him a waterproof mat next time I go away…

Baa Baa Black Sheep, Have You Any Wool?

I love summer - hazy, warm days with blue skies and warm breezes; endless hours of sunshine and glory with that promise of more to come. There is another reason I love summer. It brings with it the shearers.

I do not have a massive flock of sheep, which perhaps is the understatement of the year. The numbers once swelled to 4, but have settled at a more comfortable 3. My sheep flock originally started with 3 decrepit 'North County Mules' that I acquired from a local farmer. They had passed their breeding days and

 had the ominous mark of the red spot painted on their necks. I merrily assumed it was a flock mark to

segregate them from the others, so they could perhaps have a little more tender care in their dotage. But sadly no, it turned out to be the mark of their demise. They were due to go into the human food chain because they could no longer bare young. They were 6 years old – old for a breeding sheep, but only half way through their natural life span. I called them Flopsy, Mopsy and Cottontail. I love my sheep. They are very misunderstood animals. Yes, they do try hard to die, and yes, they do have a collective mind-set to run headlong regardless of whether they need to or not, but they are kind, gentle, sensitive and have the remarkable ability to remember a human face for eight years (don't ask me how this fact was ever ascertained…) . These 3 old ladies stayed with me for the rest of their natural life span and I loved them dearly.

It happened upon one freezing winter's day, in the winter of 2010 that I was driving along and saw a sheep. Not an uncommon occurrence in these Northern parts, however this sheep was different. To start with he was not in a field, but had lain down in the snow by the side of the road. He was young, his fleece was falling off and he was pitifully thin. He was, however, a Hebriddean – not known for their complicity. I stopped the car. I had to think. This sheep was in a bad way, there was not a chance in Hell I was going to leave him to die. I got out of my car and the sheep buggered off at high speed in the opposite direction. Now to catch a sheep in normal circumstances, they have to be either very tame, nearly dead or herded by shepherds and sheep dogs. There was just me and my car. And a long and winding road leading to nowhere. I decided to herd the sheep with my open car door, whilst driving on the wrong side of the road in icy conditions, until I could find somewhere to corner it. The sheep was quite obliging and ran much faster than I expected for a near dead animal. A rather posh Discovery rounded the corner to find me and my battered Focus driving in a manner not quite explicit in the Highway Code. He stopped, spoke a few unmentionables and drove off. Great. Now every so often, one requires a little divine intervention. I looked up to the grey and threatening sky and said to God: 'Look here, if you want this sheep to survive, you are going to have to help me out'. At which point the sheep took a turn to the right and headed into a very large windswept field. Shit. Not quite what I had in mind. However, in the corner of this field was a broken down trailer and the sheep took one look at me, and dived underneath it. Usain Bolt had nothing on me. I dived like a footballer under the trailer and grabbed its legs, pulling as hard as I could. The sheep seemed to accept its fate and played dead. I shoved him in the boot of my car, made a mental note to thank God and drove home. I named him Ragtag. He was in a really bad way. How he had survived as long as he had I'll never know. Worms dripped out in liquid muck, his ribs were like a

toast rack and he hung his head pitifully. He was wild though, and as soon as I let him out at home, he dived into a deep pile of hay and disappeared for days. I did, however, make a call to the local constabulary, to let them know I had stolen a sheep, and informed them at the same time, I wasn't giving him back. They didn't argue. Time healed, the days lengthened and Raggie, as he was affectionately known, grew and recovered. He was always a wild one, but he had an air of humility about him. There was something a bit special about that sheep.

Now the old ladies were bonded. They didn't take too kindly to a diminutive sick little boy. He hung around, trying his best to be part of their flock - which in time he was, but at that point I had no option but to buy him a companion. I needed another Hebriddean. I made a few calls and found a breeder up in Durham. Fabulous. He answered the phone and asked me whether I wanted a whole sheep or half of one. I explained that a whole one would be preferable as it needed to bond, run and play with a sheep I had. And it had to be breathing and upright. I set off in the Focus miles up North to the farm with my kids and chose a sheep. I popped him in the back of the car with the parcel shelf off and headed back. Now unfortunately, I have an issue with directions. I am totally clueless. I'm sure I have some synapses missing that other people have. I can't find my way out of a paper bag. This handicap is rectified by a SatNav. I can't live without one and often curse when riding at the horse trials and I have to navigate a course by myself. It usually ends in disaster. The problem was, I was down some country lane in County Durham and my SatNav died. There was me, my two kids and a sheep in the car. There was absolutely no chance of finding my way back. So I did what I usually do in that situation, and drove aimlessly around trying hard to get some clues. After a lifetime, I came upon Tesco's. Thank God (again). I parked up, extracted the kids from the sheep and headed in. They sold SatNavs. I didn't hesitate. I passed over the £100, blanked that bit out and set off with a rather disgruntled, large horned sheep. The passers-by did look a little closer than normal into the back of the car, as this poodle-like creature was trying his hardest to

crash his way out of the back window with a set of horns that wouldn't look out of place on a Water Buffalo. I smiled and waved, and put my foot down. Bobtail, as he was so aptly called, jumped like an antelope around the field when he was released and made himself at home.

Time passed and the ebb and flow of life resumed. Life is so short and pain lasts so long. My flock dwindled. Each little flame burns brightly in my heart. Mopsy was the last of the 3 old ladies to go and Bobtail still thrives.

I had made a promise to my children that we would have 2 pet lambs as soon as there was an opportunity. It came about that I acquired Juno and Jupiter – my two little babies. These were hand reared inside the house in nappies, and are totally adored and tame. Their life revolves around polo mints, horse treats and sheep nuts. Jupiter is a big lad with a big attitude – both are Suffolk crossed with North County Mule. Jupiter spent his formative months drinking milk like his life depended on it; sleeping like the dead; or posing like a ninja before dashing at objects at high speed to send them crashing – then would passage off – head held high and little legs prancing. He was a real stallion of a lamb. I grew suspicious. We had 'ringed' him when he first arrived and so, in theory, he had no

testicles. I remember drying him off in the kitchen and rubbing his tummy vigorously with a towel, to find a little withered scrotum in my hand, not attached to anything. 'Oh', I then exclaimed, and wondered what to do with it. I popped it on the breakfast bar whilst getting myself, the kids and the sheep ready for work / school/ a day sleeping and playing. It stared at me, a white elephant in the room. The cats looked interested... I hastily binned it.

Jupiter was, in theory, castrated but he was such a boy. I asked the vets to investigate. Peter Wright put one hand on his tummy and exhaled loudly. A testicle the size of a rugby ball lay within his body cavity. He was a man, not a boy.

Juno was a sweet little darling – absolutely angelic. I owed it to her to have a peaceful life without the amorous attentions of a  red blooded tup. Jupiter was certainly top dog. He enjoyed intimidating all other lesser mortals. It is only myself and Alan that he considers superior and he often runs to me for cuddles when life gets too much. Every other human is cannon fodder. He is the archetypal guard sheep.

 I made the decision to get him recastrated, in the vague hope that he would become a gentle, testosterone free little sheep. The 'Yorkshire Vet' film crew were

very interested in the story and rang me to ask if they could film the whole process. Wow – to be a film star! Visions of Hollywood filtered into my brain and I willingly agreed. I unashamedly admit that I was excited. The crew gave me ½ hour notice. I was sat in a café in Thirsk with my Mum when I got the call. 30 short minutes to drive 6 miles home, turn myself into Julia Roberts, and the house into a respectable dwelling rather than a farm yard. No chance. I raced back - the Focus in overdrive, skidded into the yard, fell over the kids who were to be on tele as well and needed at least 24 hours' notice to glam up, and started throwing pots and pans and general debris into cupboards. I am so glad the cameras didn't have x-ray vision. I looked a wreck and my film-star future lay in the wardrobes and drawers upstairs. It made great TV though, and Juno and Jupiter became famous. It was the start of their TV career. They are on TV again next week for Jupiter's 'de-budding'. Now as previously stated, summer brings its own duties, and one of which is shearing. I celebrate this annual event like a druid. To me, it marks a definite turning point in the seasons. In the early days, Alan and I took on the monumental task ourselves. Half a day would pass with us both taking turns to fight the sheep and

strip them bare. It was a stressful event. The sheep would end up rainbow coloured – blood red with purple spray mixed with grass stains and sweat. I called it a day. I always refused to shear the black

sheep anyhow as I couldn't judge what was skin and fleece – I swear it hurt me more than them, but the horror of drawing

blood on one of my babies was unbearable. The only positive aspect was I could get to kiss my incumbent babies noses as I let each one go. The sheep weren't impressed.

I endeavoured to find myself a shearer. A professional who could strip 100 in the time it took us to do 1. I found him in a field. As I walked over to him, with several hundred sheep bleating like deranged Buddhists monks, and a team of lads looking on sceptically, he eyed me with a glint in his eye - a Geordie glint - one of those twinkles that acts like a light to a moth. I grinned inanely and asked if he sheared sheep…

And so started a long and happy relationship with my shearer. I look forward to summer bringing with it the men whose tanned shoulders stand like girders; whose eyes twinkle in the sunshine; who take a wild 100kg sheep and gently render it motionless and

compliant; who banter and laugh and flirt, but are entirely focused on the welfare of their charges. I wish I was a sheep…

I always celebrate this event – with some girlfriends, laughter and food – it would be wrong of me to keep this ~~Adonis~~ shearer to myself. They not only shear my sheep, but trim their feet, worm them, and take great care of them. They truly are amazing

– in every sense of the word… and my sheep love them.

Hen Party

Hens are funny things. They provide hours of entertainment just by being hens. My little brood of ladies consist of the 'princesses' – an ancient collection of 'Welsummers', that are very prim and correct and do not mix too well with the 'ex-bats'. These so-called ex bat girls are the real renegades. They have survived a tortuous existence as factory farmed hens living in tiny battery cages (no, these haven't been banned, they have been made bigger, but then have been packed with more hens), and thanks to the British Hen Welfare Society, have been rescued to be re-homed. I admire their plucky little spirits and thus, they are all named after the valiant suffragettes. Sadly, their lives are short. They are bred to lay eggs then die. However, one or two hang on in there and make it to a ripe old hen age. Because of this short life span, I regularly have to restock. Alan plays hell and tries to insist I buy 'normal' hens that lay normal eggs and do normal hen things. As usual, I nod and agree, then go and do exactly what it was I had originally planned to do. I love my ex-bat suffragette ladies with their pioneering spirits.

At each rehoming, I vow to bring home the healthiest of the bunch – every time one dies, I mourn their little lives and it hurts. Every time I arrive at the rehoming centre, I head straight for the most pitiful and broken little beings and take all of these motley crew home. Invariably one is always lame – which in hen terms means it walks like John Cleese. This hen earns the honour of being called Cicely Hamilton. The scruffiest and most moth-eaten is Emily Davison, as I assume the original Emily Davison looked a little worse for wear after going under the King's horse. There is always a Lady Constance Bulwer-Lytton, an Emmeline Pankhurst, Annie Henney (Kenney, for those in the know) and so on. I confess to making up the name of Fanny Goodwill for one of my hens – there really should have been a suffragette with this name. I had to smile to myself when she ended up at the vets one day; I sat and waited for the pained expression upon the surgeon's face when they hollowed out 'Fanny Goodwill' across the packed waiting room. The vets see quite a few of my hens. These little girls come home with a long list of ailments that I know the vets will sort – well apart from the hen that swelled up, and upon being turned upside down to assess, promptly died; or the one with the badly broken leg that couldn't be saved. The vet kindly asked if I wanted to take her

little body home. I declined, but rather regretted it when the vet bill came back and there was a charge for

her incineration – Alan muttered something about the cost of roast chicken and I'm sure there was something in his outburst that sounded like 'plucking bells'… Perhaps it was the £130 charge for the wing amputation in another of the broken ladies that he was referring to.

However, these ladies live out the rest of their days in unadulterated hen luxury as is befitting for their circumstances. At one point I created a hen playground for them, as an enrichment programme to keep them entertained. Unfortunately it entertained the local rat population more, which then turned into a battle of wits of trying to out manoeuvre the rats. They, quite naturally, won. It was time to rehome them. I decided to dig them out – expecting to find half a dozen or so. As I dug, the ground seemed to move, then it opened up in fifty different places as fat rats, thin rats, big rats and small all evacuated their premises and headed out to the four winds. It was like something off 'splat-a-rat' except that I didn't splat a thing, just watched in morbid fascination as they ran over my wellies and headed for freedom. I dismantled their home and apart from an odd hardened gnarly old timer that helps himself to the odd egg now and then, they haven't returned.

 Hens love nothing more than to scrat around in the soil looking for wiggly things and discussing it at great length with their fellow compatriots. If the ground happens to be disturbed

for any reason, they are there, like mini dinosaurs, scratting and chatting and generally getting under one's feet. So, it came to the time to lay the electricity cables down for the glamping site. A relatively straight forward job for Alan and his digger - except that the pipe needed to go from our old 'cow-house' as it is so

eloquently called, down through the hen run, out through the horses' field, into the top field and then into the area that is the glamping site. This distance necessitated a  massive electric cable – as thick as my wrist, as well as two other cables that have something to do with the internet, it also required a massive trench. The hens were in hen heaven. Alan was in hen hell. He was under strict instructions to not run over any hen or turkey that was on any suicide mission. Hens dive bombed the trench, back-filled it with scratting, squawked manically, ran headless in front of the digger, feathers were ruffled, worms were consumed and finally, the trench was dug.

Not one hen lost its life. Mission accomplished. Then it rained. I'm trying hard not to mention the bit about my beautiful green hen run now resembling the Somme, claggy clay clinging like Golem onto my boots. Hens skidding and doing hand break turns on their wings as they run for their breakfast. It'll dry, the grass will grow, I will again be able to sunbathe with my feathered friends in their green and pleasant home, and the natural order of summer will resume. Hopefully.

I've got a Brand New Combine Harvester and I'll Give You The key

The world is full of rich and diverse cultures, each with its own language and idioms. This stretches to the weird and wonderful world of Yorkshire farmers. I have, out of necessity, become a

cunning linguist and now pride myself on speaking 'farmer'. I'm not great at it and I have to study hard. It is a subtle tongue that consists mostly of guttural grunts, head tilts and the odd: 'Aye.' added for flavour. To watch two specimens in full flight would be worthy of a full research grant as this language is enhanced by a plethora of mannerisms and practises: the slight head tilt in recognition of a comrade; the 'aye' as a substitute for a whole conversation; the critical, narrowed, beady eye of quiet contemplation and not least, the ability to drive down any road with their head a full 90 angle. This rather unnerving talent is in order to peer over their neighbour's hedges to assess how far (or not) the harvest is coming along. But perhaps my favourite idiom is the Yorkshire wave. It consists of one finger raised marginally off the steering wheel as a gratuitous 'Thanks'. I've adopted this myself. These hardened, tenacious, wily old -timers are a subtly friendly bunch. Their hearts are pure gold and their pockets are deep – so deep in fact that nothing ever comes out. They are very attached of each other – but they certainly do not suffer fools gladly, and new-comers are new-comers for the rest of their days. It is the archetypal rural 'old boys club'.

Part of the language idiosyncrasy is never to use proper nouns, but rely totally on a selection of pronouns – mostly 'he' but if it happens to be an inanimate object such as a tractor or Mother Nature causing issues, then the pronoun is always female. It requires a good memory bank of previous conversations to follow which 'he' is the conversation focus. These friendly bunch of farmers are usually laid back and like nothing better than to 'chew the fat'- as Alan so eloquently puts it. We have a regular bunch of lads that frequent our farm. All arrive in a work premise. I sometimes slightly wince at the idea they all charge an hourly fee, and they all chew the fat for a good many of those hours – no wonder there is no money in farming!

At certain times of the year there is a definite competitive feel in the air. The elusive and craved for badge of honour is worn with pride if you happen to be the farmer that completes (or even starts) an annual event first. These events make up the farming calendar and consist of ploughing, power harrowing, drilling, rolling, hay, haylage or silage making. Perhaps the biggest prize of all goes to the farmer that cranks up the combine harvester first. The cut-off date for this unofficial competition is the 'The

 Great Yorkshire Show' (our annual celebration of all things rural). Farmers at this event can be identified by both place and dress. All are found congregating either by the cattle, sheep or pig sections, or near the new machinery. Their uniform consists of

either blue or green Dickies overalls, white show coats, or if they are off duty, then their attire is the statutory checked shirt, trousers and either Hoggs or Jodhpur boots. Pockets of trousers usually bulge with rolls of slightly oil-coated £20 notes, keys, ...al detritus. The older boys have heads adorned with grease covered flat caps. Their hands are like shovels and their hearts are aglow. It is the coming together ...the west wind has carved their ruddy complexions and the rain and sun has weathered them. But I love them one and all.

Alan is the finest example of all things Yorkshire Farmer. His bright blue eyes shine like jewels in his weathered and sunburnt face. His hands are like spades - all ingrained and rough and can build and mend and make and do absolutely anything. He speaks his own language 'Si thi' (Hi); 'Lal Fergie' (our old and little, grey Fergie tractor), 'Beyates' (boots) and 'See est a wither' (see you later) and – my favourite: 'The year's buggered' (referring in his candid tongue to the fact that once the winter barley is harvested in July, the best of the summer is over and winter is on its way). He loves nothing more than playing on and tinkering with his beloved collection of decrepit and slightly less decrepit tractors and farm machinery.

All is calm through the seasons on our farm as the green, sea-like waves of barley heads move and whisper in the early summer sun. But then the tension in the air rises just a touch when the first of the winter barley starts to dry and yellow. I like to listen to the tell-tale popping of billions of grains drying and bowing as the sun evaporates the swollen rain soaked heads. I ride around the set-aside strips and quietly contemplate the ebb  and flow of nature's clock. The wind blows dry and the corn turns. Then, like a captain holding his army to rank, Alan takes out the moisture tester. The air turns momentarily blue as the digital gadget outsmarts the mechanical age. The corn is tested. Breath is held. Waiting.

Waiting. Then that magical figure appears – less than 14% moisture and we're on. Phone calls follow and then fellow farmer Pete appears in his gargantuan, growling, clanking, ancient combine. It's 20 years old if it's a day. It gobbles the barley heads and spits out the straw and clunks and grinds and snorts. But it works. The boys turn back to their childhood as they harvest the crop and play like schoolboys with their machinery. Alan drives the tractor and trailer to gather the corn as it fires like a waterfall out of the combine. Back and forth they go, row upon row of waving barley lies as straw on the stubble. I too feel that rush of adrenaline. Stubble fields. Endless miles of galloping.

We never win the competition. Our soil is clay and holds the damp. The boys with the sandy soil always win. Their heads are held that touch higher. Their combines that much newer. But our crops yield. The droughts don't starve our fields. Our fields are home and beautiful. Through the seasons the ripening corn host deer. The buzzard cry overhead. The rabbits scarper and the kestrels hunt in our waving, dreaming corn.

Yorkshire's best kept secret – the Morndyke Mini Shop

Football just isn't my bag. I managed about 10 seconds – was marginally amused by the name of one Brazilian player, so made a few un pc comments to myself that made me giggle, then was bored. Apparently I have the sense of humour of a 13 year old boy… according to my adult 12 year old daughter….

I prefer cake. So with this in mind I have revamped the Morndyke Mini Shop. I've even had a sign made by Alpha Signs in Thirsk (who are fab and do all my signage) to say 'shop' with an arrow. Not many people use my shop. In fact, it's probably only me. It's one of Yorkshire's best kept secrets.

It's starting to be obvious that I use the shop a little too much. I was talking to one gentleman today whom I hadn't seen for about 6 weeks and I swear I caught him talking to my stomach rather than my face. No degree in psychology was needed to work out what he was thinking.

Anyhow, back to the shop. I now sell a selection of the most amazing flapjacks ever made – from Yorkshire flapjacks. (Don't ask me how I know they are amazing…☺)

I'm also stocking Yorkshire honey, Yorkshire jam, Yorkshire fruitcake, Yorkshire Yorkshire Parkin (☺), Yorkshire biscuits, Yorkshire Apple juice, Yorkshire another drink thingy – which has a weird name but tastes nice, Yorkshire crisps, Yorkshire posy, Yorkshire my book. Oh yeah, and Tesco bbq coals and Choc n Choc luxury farmyard chocolates. Not from Yorkshire. Sadly. Trying hard now not to make any un pc jokes about allowing in products from foreign lands…. ie across the borders from non-Yorkshire counties. I like Yorkshire.

So, if you happen to also be bored of football and fancy a nibble, then come round and eat something Yorkshire. Please.

Ducklings at Springtime. Spring has sprung

Spring has sprung at Morndyke. It's certainly the time of year for new life – it's springing up every where! The countryside is flooded with babies. It's about this time when the ducklings hatch – I love the quote from a favourite childhood book of my kids: 'All the Places to Love', that describes ducklings as 'tiny tumbles of leaves'. They certainly are. Even the hardened farmers and fisherman's eyes soften at the site of these innocent little darlings. God help any cat or fox that gets too close. These men are maternal! Well that's until the ducklings grow and don't look quite so sweet – more juicy. Poor little loves. It's not great when you're a vegetarian living in a world of carnivores. In the mean time these little angels have many guardian angels looking over them.

Our lake is cold. And deep….

Our lake is cold. And deep. And has a chequered past. I'd love to know it's full history.

It started life as a clay pit for making bricks hundreds of years ago. Just after the war the council tipped their rubbish in it and it shrank from 4 acres to 2. Occasionally in the past, Alan would report strange bubbles and glugs coming from its depths. The fish love it though- all ten thousand or so of them. Even the legend that is a 28 1/2 pound carp that sends fishermen into night sweats and brakes rods and lines. He rules the lake like a God. He has been landed and weighed once by two men. I feel slightly uncomfortable watching Alan standing near waist deep in the cold waters knowing that the beast is in there….

Over the decades the silt has built up to create a false bottom that is scarcely deep. The water alone is about 12 foot deep in places, but go through that silt layer and sink forever into Hades- or so I used to tell the kids to stop them playing in it. It's turned into a mysterious force of nature that deserves deep respect in our household. A bit like the bottom bit of bananas that my father told me were poisonous. I still eye them warily when I eat a banana and no hell or high water will make me eat them- just in case….

Capote gets wet. Again.

What a difference a day makes. HEAT. The date is April 20th 2018. Has Spring arrived? Is this a temporary respite from the winter deluges? Capote certainly hopes so. I think he has shrunk from too many soakings.

RAIN AND RAIN AND RAIN

First Capote got wet with rain. He then found a muddy patch (not difficult) and rolled in it. He got wetter. And muddier.

Then Capote was wet with sea water- we went to the beach at a Marske, and the sea was huge. I like to paddle and swim. Capote doesn't.   We   paddled   and   almost   swam. Then the sun shone.

Today Capote was wet with sweat. He was then was wet from his shower and hair wash. He sort of likes his shower. He hates the heat. He's Spanish. He's modelling Tresemme shampoo and conditioner here, finished with a touch of Moroccan oil for that 'after salon glow'. His hair is shinier than mine. Think I need to use it.

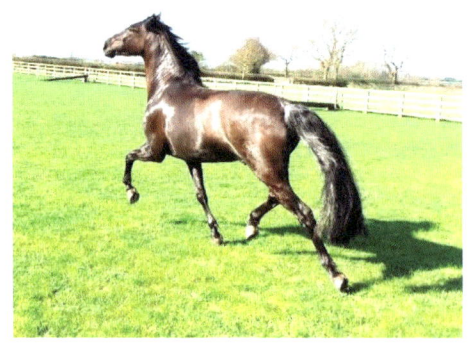

William Wordsworth at Morndyke

Shepherds' Huts

I wandered lonely as a cloud

That floats on high o'er vales and hills,

When all at once I saw a crowd,

A host, of golden daffodils;

Beside the lake, beneath the trees,

Fluttering and dancing in the breeze.

I reckon **Wordsworth** must have known a thing or two about daffodils, and possibly a thing or two about Morndyke. Our daffodils here are spectacular and well worth a viewing. The birds in the dawn chorus are just beautiful too.

Why not just come for a wander – it's all here for free! See all, hear all, pay nowt – I wonder if that's a Wordsworth quote too… He must have been an honorary Yorkshireman. If not I think I'll make him one…

I swear we are related to the Durrells.

Is it only us that constantly ends up being 'found' by things? The latest find is Bramble Jack.

To cut a long story short, the cold and wet Tuesday last week was no exception. I had finally managed to stuff the car with kids and coats on our way out to an appointment (late) when I happened to glance up and noticed a grey ball laying in the stable yard. So, hand break on, jump out of the car- followed by the kids and their general detritus, and approached said grey ball. It looked up at me and didn't move. So, like a whirlwind, I scooped it up and my entourage followed me back into the house to check it and assess it and feed it - 'It' being a juvenile feral pigeon.

It now lives in Anna's room. They are in love. Bramble Jack takes residence on either Anna's shoulder, Anna's head or the branch that Anna has installed in her bedroom. He eats a lot. And poos a lot. He's learning how to Snapchat through the process of Osmosis. He squeaks when hungry, is starting to learn to fly without crash landing, and thinks he's Anna's baby.

So does Anna.

The tale of a goose named Lucy

Lucy, dear little Lucy – the amount of stress and grief you have given me is immeasurable.

The day came last week when I decided that the three different types of antibiotics I was using were no longer working and you were completely blind in your one remaining eye, I knew the kindest thing to do was the hardest decision to make.

I cried; I cuddled you; I photographed your last morning as the sun warmed your back.

After 30 years of you being you, I was ready to call time on your little life. With a broken heart, I called out the vet for the umpteenth and final time.

He studied you, examined you then watched your little waddle. Then he turned to me and told me that you were happy and that being blind wasn't a reason to die. I could have kissed him, but kissed you instead. I now have to carry you to your food and water three times a day and put your beak in it and watch you eat, drink, wash and play in your bath. I love you little Lucy, you are worth every muddy footprint I have on my work clothes and every disapproving look I get when I run into work late on a daily basis.

Bless you little Lucy, I hope you live for another 30 years, but just wish you'd do it quicker so I don't actually lose my job.

Auction Virgin

I went to my first ever **auction** on Tuesday. I found some old pots that I thought would look fab on the glamping site, so I decided to bid.

Well not being your 'normal' kind of girl, I tackled this like a headless chicken. I don't do subtle. I was so busy chatting to the old folks around me about missing the bidding by chatting, that I nearly missed my bidding – much to Alan's disgust.

I then threw my arm up with great enthusiasm when I worked out that my Lot 16 was up. Blimey, the auctioneer rattled the cash figures out like a machine gun, so by the time my arm came back down he had reached £35! My limit was £20. Alan was horrified. An old bloke won thank God.

I was down, but not out. It was time to act sharpish. After even less subtle flirting, me and the bloke struck a deal and I paid £20 for nearly the lot. He kept one. Result. They'll look great planted up with geraniums in the summer. Alan has banned me from auctions.

Wedding Anniversary ... with a difference...

It was my **wedding anniversary** last Monday. It goes without saying that Alan forgot. He's a Yorkshire farmer after all.

Admittedly this unromantic side of him always niggles me a bit. I got flowers – off a gorgeous friend. I got a card – off my Mum. I thought about it all day, and then thought I'd buy a nice meal for tea. After all, lead by example etc etc. Well that was the plan.

4pm, Anna got home from school. I ran the idea by her and we both headed off to Tesco's. We spent ages choosing Alan's favourite food, pudding and nice things, which naturally led us to the 'poor person☹' section in the fridge area. There we both saw the 'live oysters' in a polythene bag, just sitting there minding their own business in the cold.

Anna and I exchanged glances and then grabbed them. After a quick discussion we headed for the fish section and asked for all their mussels and any other live food. It was going to be a rare old feast – or so the man thought.

I got home and told Alan about his beautiful dinner, but added on the tiny extra bit about it not actually going according to plan – we had shopping bags full of live shellfish. Live shellfish that were destined to be boiled alive or eaten alive. Not on my watch. Alan stood with open mouth and shook his head in disbelief. His gorgeous dinner would have to wait for another day- we were off to the seaside to 'Free Willy' or free three bags full of mussels and oysters.

Alan has banned me from Tesco's. Again.

The chaos of the cows continues

So the cows have been turned out for the summer grazing, and all was well with the world. That is until Alan rang me. Apparently one of 'them red heifers' (who incidentally haven't been heifers for a couple of years, but the name stuck) had calved at Robin's. So, the usual drill ensued – jump in the truck, find the calf, inject it against ecoli, castrate it if it's a bull calf, and check whether it had been drinking. In other words, **chaos reigns supreme with the cows at Morndyke.**

We found the calf. It was cold and shaky and on its own. Mum was nowhere near it. It didn't look good. I told Alan that it had to come home but I was suspicious. A mummy very rarely abandons their baby. I asked Alan to drive around the field. Then I saw it. Another calf. This one was stronger and mum was more interested. We had no choice but to bring the whole family home so the weaker baby would have a chance of bonding with the cow.

That was no mean feat carrying a calf each across a large field in a way that the mother cow would follow. It's amazing how heavy a new born calf is over a 30 acre rough field. Finally we had all three of them loaded and brought them back. Little Bambi and Biba are now doing well and mum has worked out she has two little babies to love. All's well with the world…

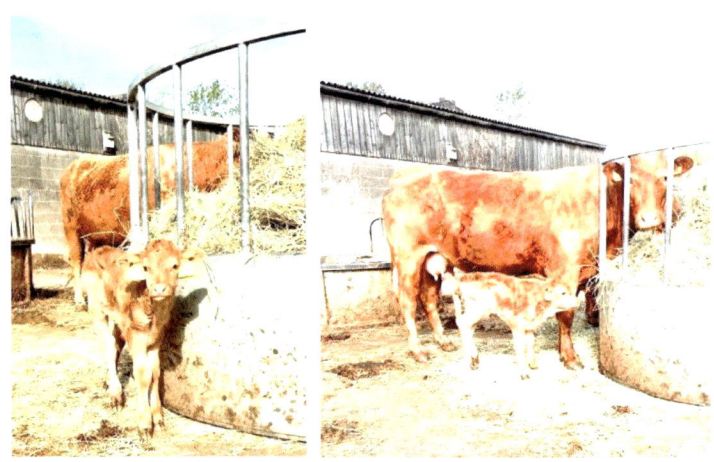

Barbels to basking sharks. Fishing at Morndyke

One of the good things about our shepherds' huts are that they are right next to our lake – perfect if you like fishing.

We have an eclectic selection of fish, which I'm afraid I know nothing about, as I don't fish and have no inclination to do so. I don't know my **barbels from my basking sharks** – well ok, I might have an idea about that one, and I'm assured that basking sharks don't like our silted still waters. However, the fish we do have are: Roach; Carp – mirror, common, grass; Tench- golden & green; Barbel; Chub.

Apparently this is a good thing and they attract different types of fishermen, who need different types of kit and rods and thingys. I'm convinced they all catch the same fish, that must be a) very greedy, b) very dim c) very numb. The other 9999 fish must just coerce this fish into catching the bait. I've known classes of children   just   like   this…. Here is a fisherman catching the said fish for the umpteenth time that day. Think it must be full to bursting by now.

CAUTION: THIS IS FOR WOMEN ONLY

(My gift to you)

It's THAT time of year again. Scantily clad, sun-kissed, broad-shouldered men tenderly handling innocent and trusting creatures AKA ***shearing time***

I unashamedly admit to lustful thoughts every time the guys turn up. Who wouldn't? I think even the blesséd Mother Theresa (God rest her soul) would have had a sneaky glance from under that tea towel. I can't decide whether it is the toned golden physique, the gentle caressing hands, or that wicked little twinkle in the eye that sends my knees weak and my heart aflutter. I've given up trying to carve my virtuous pathway to heaven, and have no intentions of confessionals. I think the priest would go blind if I admitted all my wicked thoughts!

So as a way of penance, I thought it only right and proper to share this experience with the rest of the nation's girls. Here follows a storyboard of pictures. I will leave each one for you to right your captions either in your head or under the photos. Indeed create your own fantasy story if you wish. I know I do….

I think the expression on the sheep's faces tell its own tale, but I'm not expecting many of you to notice that there are indeed sheep in the pictures…

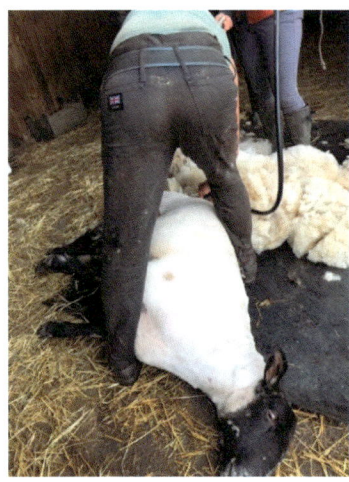
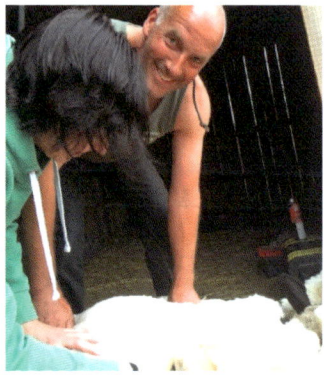

Breckenbrough Horse Trials.

Today I was going to compete at Breckenbrough Horse Trials, but it's rained. Then rained some more. I'd need flippers and a snorkel and I don't look great in a bikini, so inevitably it's been cancelled.

Instead, I'm doing this, I'm playing with cows. Well, herding cows. OK, convincing cows they want a trip in the cow fairground ride. They don't.

It's that time of year again when the legend that is Dan-the-foot-trimming-man comes and offers our girls their annual manicure and pedicure. Even Hercules the bull gets a go – he's in touch with his feminine side. The girls all come out clean and shiny toed. I come out covered in shit.

Please don't rain next year.

Damsels in distress at Morndyke Shepherds' Huts

One of the great things about running a glamping site is meeting the clients. All kinds of people come through our gates bringing with them all sorts of personalities and stories. I love it. Some become good friends, some prefer to keep themselves to themselves and some love to chat. Without exception all are lovely. It's great to meet such a diverse range of people. I especially love the ones that don't leave all their washing up for the cleaners….

One of the mildly amusing aspects of meeting new people is watching Alan meet new people. He's a Yorkshire farmer through and through, his friends are all drawing pensions and are equally rural. He does however, run a very successful fencing business where he ensures great estates are securely fenced and priceless equines kept in their place. He's a charmer with the ladies and will bend over backwards to ensure his female clients are happy and well serviced (presumably not in the biblical sense, although one would have more sense that to question this…). The men get an equally good job done, it's just that those blue eyes don't twinkle and the conversation has more grunting in it.

Alan loves a **damsel in distress**, he blossoms in their peril. Theses damsels usually appear in threes and all are barely out of their teens. The first three appeared on our site in the late and very wet Spring. Like a flash, Alan was there. He lit their fire, he helped with the ladder, he even put up their gazebo that they had brought. Out came the drill and screws, and cheeky grin. It was a wild and blustery night. Early the next morning he was there mending the flailing tarpaulin whilst the ladies slept on, oblivious. I think it was the greeting he got of young ladies in bras that sealed his unyielding service.

Three more have turned up today. From London. Lovely young girls that are new to lighting fires and cooking outside. Like a flash, Alan is there, the barbecue lit, the ladder in place, the instructions given with a smile and a twinkle. Alan loves the glamping site. He loves the people it brings. Especially if they come in packs of three.

Harvest time is here again

Its *that* time of year again: Pete's old combine has been dusted off, its rat-chewed wires have been taped up with a bit of duck tape (incredibly versatile stuff) to stop the old girl firing. A bit of grease has been applied lovingly to some ancient cranking parts, and we have commissioned it to harvest the first of our crops- the winter barley.

Now obviously, due to the nature of Yorkshire farmers, there is always a negative to everyone else's positive. Earlier in the year, it was the head shaking and long exhalations – undeniable stress at the relentless rain that stopped the crops being sown on time. 'I don't know, I've niver known out like it!' Alan would mutter as the rain lashed the windows and soaked all in sundry to the skin. ' The year's buggered!' was a mantra that was expressed on a very regular basis.

Then came the sun – it was ok to begin with and I even witnessed an odd spring in the Hoggs boots as Alan went about his daily business. But the sun continued. Now to me, it is fantastic- a proper summer of my bygone days. Admittedly all the watering is a pain in the arse, but it's a small price to pay for the glorious sunshine and incredible sunsets that leave the sky touched in a hue of pink.

The head shaking is back. And the stress. 'I can remember in 1976, it were just like this…' followed by another sharp intake of breath and an exhale of desperation. Admittedly it is a huge problem for some farmers in some places, but not for us. Clay soil means the ground holds the water, our fields are holding their own for now. They are still green and the grass is still growing for the cattle to eat. But for Alan it is clearly a source of potential negativity.

The NorthWest have a hose pipe ban. Alan now regularly reminds me that we are next- more head shaking and grimaces as he describes the chore of watering cans. Some poor sod somewhere has had to cull his herd of cattle due to lack of food. I can see Alan visibly curl as he walks around with his head a little lower. 'I've niver known out like it!'. Our cattle positively gleam in the sun soaked green fields.

And now it's harvest. The winter barley is as dry as snuff – perfect in fact. Low moisture count means a great crop. The field has yielded well due to the early rains and then sunshine days. The straw is crisp and golden, fluffy and soft. It's the most perfect we've had for a long time. But I know 'the year is buggered.' now the combine had been and the straw baled.

As we bask in relentless sunshine of halcyon days that my children will remember: summers lasting forever and winters cold and snowy, Alan shakes his head and joins in the camaraderie of his counterparts. He loves it. It makes him Alan – an archetypal Yorkshire farmer.

The rains will come, the year will progress, the second cut of silage will happen at some point, but each will give the opportunity for that secret Yorkshire head shake and long exhalation of breath as the old boys exchange stories of hardship and gloom. It makes them happy as they tinker away with their duck tape and grease.

Daisy's ExPLODition

The world is full of remarkable people – sometimes it's hard to see, but they are out there, hiding amongst the ordinary.

One such lady I have had the privilege to meet right next to us here at Morndyke, is Daisy on her explodition aka **Daisy's ExPLODition**

I happened to be driving passed our fields next to the Jaipur Spice, and had to do a double take. Our verge had suddenly been filled with the most beautiful gypsy caravan and 2 amazing Belgian Draught horses. Not one to miss an opportunity to meet a horse, I screeched to a halt, reversed up, abandoned the car and introduced myself. These horses are incredible- great muscle machines and rare too. Proper working horses.

It turned out that this most remarkable lady is travelling from Banbury (in Oxfordshire), to Falkirk – to the iconic 30 foot high Kelpies, and back again. The purpose of such a journey is to raise awareness and donations for The Brain Tumour charity. Daisy happens to be in her 70s. It's a 5-month, 1000 mile round trip. Olive and Arthur are the engines of this trek. Daisy writes a blog on Facebook too – it's well worth following her. How many of us, when we reach our 70s, (if indeed we do), will be hiding out there, amongst the ordinary, living an extraordinary life?

There's a large part of me that envies Daisy. To have the freedom to fly where the wind takes you, with your animals as your constant companions. To stay snug and warm, with a wood burning stove and a comfy deep bed. To live by the day and not stress about tomorrow. To have flowers in your hair, to live and love and laugh.. sigh….

I've been sizing up Capoté and the Shepherds' Huts…

 My sister says I'm a dreamer. I think she could be right.

The Mystery of the Missing Hair Bands

It's a strange one. At night, my routine doesn't alter much – being a woman of a certain age, I climb into bed and take my watch off and take the hair band off my wrist that I'd put there earlier from my ponytail. Yet something happens between the hours of going to bed and getting dressed in the morning – my hair band disappears.

Now it's an old house – at least 150 years old and probably more. Nobody actually knows it's definitive age as there aren't any records. Old houses often have strange happenings and it doesn't really bother me too much, it's just a bit inconvenient trying to find a new hair band, when I'm running late (always), that still works. It also costs money, but not a huge amount so I let it go. It's just a mystery. It's just strange how the poltergeist has a penchant for used and probably (guaranteed) slightly smelly rubber that has my hair entangled in it. Oh well, that's life.

The odd thing is that I often discover chewed and slightly fishy hair bands in the cats food bowl. I confess that in desperate times I have fished them out and bunged them in my hair thinking that as my locks are so thick anyway, and probably (definitely) full of new and interesting life forms that belong in the stable yard rather than in a head of hair, nobody will actually notice a soggy, bedraggled rubber band that smells of fish.

So the question is, who is the culprit? There's a choice of two:

Two innocent purr machines;

Two 'Lady and the Tramp' Siamese;

Two highly intelligent, full of character, hilarious and loving vocal pussy cats;

But only one kleptomaniac.

One is hyperactive, vocal, has a fetish for aluminium, but generally brings back the screwed up tin foil balls in order to play fetch. However, has a secret love of Nerf bullets and would move heaven and earth to pinch one. But again, the best game in the world is fetch. He just can't help himself. Lightening quick, attention seeking paws and meows alert me to his antics. It just can't be Kiki, he just isn't subtle enough.

So that leaves one. One called Khufu – the kleptomaniac cat. One autistic pussy with a penchant for rubber. And plastic bags. One little fellow that has been back and forth to the vets for months due to sickness. Teeth have been removed in case they were the culprit. Sickness pills given. Antibiotics dished out. Still no abating the howls and vomit that periodically filled the house.

The last visit to the vet was filmed for the 'Yorkshire Vet'. It felt like old times with Dave Terry there filming. This time Peter was on the case though. X-rays were taken of practically the whole of Khufu. And the truth was out. Surgery was booked, the film crew were brought in, vets and nurses were on hand for 'Operation Khufu, the kleptomaniac cat' . 15 hair bands were extracted from Khufu's tummy. 15 soggy, fishy, slimy hair bands will be on national television any time soon. And one sore and sorrowful sheepish moggy.

Oh Khufu, we love you. You muppet.

The Twilight Zone

They say that a change is as good as a rest. The jury is out, to put it mildly. It feels more like purgatory. But at least I think I've earned some browny points on the 'Being a Good Mother' front. To say that I am a rabbit in the headlights is an understatement. The reason is this:

I'm currently queuing to embark on a bus. Nothing too unusual about that, except that this bus is parked inside an arena. The NEC in Birmingham to be exact. The bus has no destination and no windows either. It is big and black and red, with 'Republic of Games' written on its side in a jaunty prepubescent font. It is parked in the middle of the National Gaming Convention. The EGX.

I'm here because of my son, who happens to be into gaming and computing- again an understatement. I recently sold my beloved Freelander to pay for the parts of a PC for him to build. He talks in a language I don't understand. I'm sure he's turning into a cave dweller- I guess it's good practise for male adulthood.

I'm silently praising myself for leaving Alan at home. I think it might have actually finished him off. I have instead continued my collection of 'Good Mother' points by suggesting that my ex-husband – my children's father, comes instead. After all, he is the person responsible for giving Thomas this particular 'gaming' gene.

The Freelander thing was a bit of a Hustle moment to be honest. I sort of feel guilty. Almost. Poor Alan. He bought me a Freelander to pull my trailer and put it in his name. After a while I convinced him to transfer it into my name. He did. I've just sold it back to him for £1000 to buy Thomas these computer bits. The thing is my 13 year old car is about to fail it's MOT as it's a little bit rusty. I think I'll need the Freelander back....

I'm surrounded by men and not the sort I am used to. Gaming men. I think they've branched off the Tree of Life and are running parallel to Homo Sapiens. They certainly all look similar. I think they all dwell in caves too by the look of their complexions.

Naturally the train was late- it took us four hours to get here. Four hours home too. Seven hours here at the NEC. I'm considering it a life experience- an extreme sport in endurance and stimulation-overload and noise and lights and general Hell on Earth. The life force is being sapped from me. What's worrying me most is that Thomas wants to come next year too.

Hiding for a while in the extortionately priced cafe, I ate pizza and sorbet – £40 for 2. I survived for a while there until this bus thing called. I was the 'queue girl' whilst the others did 'stuff' and spent my money. I'm queuing and rocking and quietly shaking. My bladder is full and my brain is fried. It's been 40 looong minutes standing in this queue. It's on a promise for another 10 – I can't wait. Roll on next year.

I think my finest hour today was the grandiose fall I did in the centre of the whole convention. Thank God I'd found the toilet first.

I'd lost the will to live after 5 long hours of intense screen overload coming at me from all angles. At that point I had no choice, I made my escape. Bolting like a fox from a covert for the comfort of a bean bag I spotted at 50 feet, I didn't actually notice the raised platform. Oh boy was it a good one. Usually a fall like that is from the back of a horse. No, not I the dainty girl trip, oh no, it was the full-frontal, arms-flailing, lion-tripping-up-an-elephant type of fall. In public. In the NEC. With an audience. At least the Earth trembling vibrations I created were drowned out by the intense blaring of electronic music and technology – one blessing at least. Well that's another high point of the day.

Anna has disowned me. I think I need to go home.

The joyous day continued with the train journey home. Remind me next time to not travel to Birmingham when Sheffield Wednesday are playing an away game there against Aston Villa. And all of Sheffield embark on the same train as the one we valiantly ran to catch. I think they might have won.

The day continued in the Twilight Zone of twisted reality when I received my first ever 1 star review from a customer who hasn't actually been. She's called Kimberley. I suspect Victoria Wood knew her. 'I'm looking for my friend, She's called Kimberley, have you seen her?' is stuck in my head. Well no, actually I haven't. As she's not been. At all.

She booked to come for New Year's Eve but has cancelled a couple of times, she's rung up and she's text too – and huffed and puffed, and was immensely put out by the £20 charge for her dogs. When I pointed out that perhaps she ought to find somewhere else, she was obviously and clearly most offended, and felt the need to share her hurt, her anger and her general dissatisfaction with several booking agents that she hadn't actually used. Classic Victoria Wood material if you ask me. At least I saw the funny side. Almost. Perhaps today is just another one of those 'Quantum Leap' s for those of us old enough to remember the cult TV show.

Maybe the final straw of this alternative reality that I find myself in, was when I arrived home (at 10pm – a 16 hour day of the bizarre , the weird and the sadly not so wonderful,) to the revelation made by Alan, that in my absence a dear fisherman (as witnessed by my mother) had seen the need to take a shit in the narrow passageway that is part of, and leads to, my stable yard.

My beautiful, clean, well kept area, my holy grail, my sanctuary. I think that this one act perhaps sums up better than any words can, my day. There are strange forces afoot. I'm glad it's nearly tomorrow – I think I'm ready for it.

The Sheep Collector

There is nothing more Yorkshire than the Nidderdale Show. Set in the beautiful dales village of Pateley Bridge, it serves as a pilgrimage the the regions sheep farmers, and is followed shortly after by Masham sheep fair (which borders on the caricature, it is so Yorkshire).

It was my first time at Nidderdale, and it exceeded expectations. Pen upon pen of sheep stretched out in front of me, sheep shearers primed their blades, farmers fluffed up their proverbial feathers, donning their white coats and flat caps. There was certainly a competitive edge in the air.

Wensleydale stood next to Swaledale, who was beside Dalesbred and Masham. The iconic areas of this mighty county lay spread like a map of sheep in front of me. Each area proud of its own sheep breed. Each farmer casting a critical eye over horn and fleece and leg.

I love them all, each woolly bleating bundle of joy, whose fleeces have been groomed and dyed and oiled and trimmed. I have my favourites: the docile Suffolks with their soft eyes and relaxed ears, their great big backs and stocky legs are my sheep of choice. Their crossed breeds happen to be lovely too.

Perhaps the biggest pull for me are the pens of 'fat lambs' – as they are so daintily named. Young little lambs, about 5 months old, are penned up in groups to be shown before slaughter. It makes me feel such a huge conflict of interest. Doe eyes and trusting souls of nature's youth stare up at me. But I know their fate.

It was one such pen that called to me. Situated in a corner and full of young lambs, was a pen that I made a beeline for. I've no idea why. Sheep surrounded me from all angles, but 2 brown-faced, Suffolk-cross-Welsh sheep, mixed with a load of texels, caught my heart. I cupped their faces and stroked their heads, their little muzzles reached up to be kissed. They'd stolen my show.

Two little boys stood by the pen with their mother – the farmer's wife. I spoke some Yorkshire to break the ice and asked casually about these two lambs. Both castrated males, both played with by the boys, both loved, but both destined for slaughter. Aged five months old already, their culling date was close. I had no choice, I made my move. Working on the hearts of the kids, I pulled on their emotions. No, apparently they didn't want their little sweet darlings being brutally killed and eaten – as it so happened…. I had sealed the lambs' fate and so had intwined it with mine.

The main problem, I knew, was going to be men. The farmer looked at me like I was an impossible question. Puzzled, bemused, perplexed and incredulous, he was lost for words. The upturned sad eyes of his very young boys did the trick, and the sheep were mine. The first hurdle was cleared. The next one was going to be a little more tricky….

I hid the sheep purchase from Alan for a few days – I was on a promise. No more animals. Ever. Period. 'Ok. No problem.' I lied. So I broached the subject – and hit a wall. I wondered if he'd notice if I just sneaked them home. After all these two did look similar ish to Juno and Jupiter, but were just half the size and had different coloured faces. What could possibly go wrong?

The trouble was, was my plan of transport. I had had no problem transporting sheep in the boot of my car in the past, but this farmer was a professional with high standards and a good knowledge of the law, and the years of cavalier attitudes had long since passed. There was no way round it, I needed Alan, his truck and beast box. I had some serious work to do. I began to get to work at once.

So we all set off to the Knaresborough sheep farm with my kids in tow. Thomas, in a fog of virtual reality – having been extracted from his cave dwelling underworld of screens and games: 'Sheep? What? Huh? Whose? Do I have to?' Etc. Anna – forever the backstreet driver, 'It's down there, I told you so, don't you know anything? etc etc', with rolling eyes and sighs and huffs and the endless life experience of her 13 long years. It's lucky I brought them along, God only knows how I ever managed before them…

Finally the Roman Gods were appeased and my newly named sheep: Janus and Pluto came home. It's a tradition I started with Jupiter and Juno- name the sheep after Roman deities. God knows why. I think I'll need female sheep next- I'm running out of pronounceable male names. My flock is now 5. Jupiter, my massive Herculean Roman-chief God-sheep ran off and fell over with the shock of it all when he encountered these lesser mortals. He had to run to me for mummy hugs and comfort. Juno, his gentle and oh-so-hungry Goddess sheep friend looked slightly perplexed but found that it didn't affect her appetite. Bobtail scarpered. The horses played and snaked and chased, until the novelty wore off. Tara didn't bother. The dust settled and the comfort of chaos resumed.

Even Dad's dog found the whole thing fun.

Printed in Poland
by Amazon Fulfillment
Poland Sp. z o.o., Wrocław